Conditions That Support Transfer for Change

Valerie H. Moye

SkyLight

PROFESSIONAL DEVELOPMENT

Arlington Heights, Illinois

Conditions That Support Transfer for Change
Published by SkyLight Professional Development
2626 S. Clearbrook Dr., Arlington Heights, IL 60005-5310
800-348-4474 or 847-290-6600
Fax 847-290-6609
info@skylightedu.com
http://www.skylightedu.com

Creative Director: Robin Fogarty
Managing Editor: Barbara Harold
Editor: Barb Lightner
Book Designer: Donna Ramirez
Cover Designer: David Stockman
Production Supervisor: Bob Crump

ISBN 1-57517-043-4

2095-V
Item number U1524

Z Y X W V U T S R Q P O N M L K J I H G F E D C
06 05 04 03 02 01 00 99   15 14 13 12 11 10 9 8 7 6 5 4 3

Contents

The Missing Link

The artist transfers color and form to canvas and creates an image that reflects what has been learned vicariously and through formal schooling. The builder transfers materials and learned skills to create a building that originally was envisioned through the architect's blueprint. The information highway was built upon a foundation of transferred electronic wizardry that conveys knowledge to all parts of our world. Even the story that the dancer portrays through movement is a product of transfer. We have come to expect transfer, "the carry over or generalization of learned response from one situation to another" (Merriam-Webster 1980, 1231), as an essential process for changing and improving our world.

The construct of transfer has the greatest implications for educational leaders when related to educational reform initiatives. After all, the call for change in education has been widespread. In the past dozen years, Americans have "investigated and bemoaned the quality, the structure, and the purposes of their schools" (McLaughlin and Shepard with O'Day 1995, xi). Americans have united in the conviction that schools must improve *what* is taught, *how* it is taught, and the *degree to which students learn* what is taught. Fullan and Stiegelbauer linked reform initiatives to desired improvements by stating that the purpose of educational reform is "to help schools accomplish their goals more effectively by replacing some structures, programs, and/or practices with better ones" (1991, 15).

Despite sincere and well-intended efforts, educational reform has remained mostly an elusive goal. Since the turn of the century, numerous educational reforms have responded to widespread calls for change. But, as Cuban asked, "How can it be that so much school reform has taken place over the last century and yet so little has changed?" (1988, 341). Several studies of school reform efforts searched for possible answers to this question and revealed what has gone wrong with most school reform efforts. Huberman and Miles (1984) examined twelve case studies of large-scale school innovations and found that success was directly related to the amount and quality of assistance that was provided to those implementing the reform. The Rand Change Agent Study extensively examined projects that received federal funding and found that in many instances funding did not make a difference. However, this study found that successful projects were those that provided effective staff development that included "ongoing assistance, structures that promoted collegiality, concrete training and follow-through, and principal support and encouragement" (McLaughlin 1991, 79). Fullan (1990) agreed that successful reform is dependent on staff development. By considering transfer as the desired outcome of staff development, one can see how the question of transfer becomes an overarching theme that links professional growth to school reform.

Staff development, "those processes that improve the job-related knowledge, skills, or attitudes of school employees" (Sparks and Loucks-Horsley 1990, 5), is crucial to increasing student achievement. Time has been devoted to staff development efforts; yet, sufficient evidence of transfer has eluded those who expect that staff development will lead to necessary changes in education. A recent survey of principals from eight school divisions in Virginia documented the premise that most staff development efforts do not transfer to classroom practices (Moye 1996). Slightly more than 85 percent of the surveyed principals reported that staff development effectively altered classroom practices *only 50 percent or less of the time.* This is not a good return on the investment of time that goes toward staff development initiatives. If staff development is critical to reforms that focus on increased student achievement, then clearly the issue of transfer is worthy of close scrutiny.

The Challenge

Major reform initiatives in America are concerned with improving the quality of education available to students throughout the United States. The proposed building blocks for improvement are high standards for student learning, high standards for teaching, high-quality teacher preparation and professional development, aggressive recruitment of able teachers, rewards for teacher knowledge and skill, and schools organized for student and teacher learning (National Commission on Teaching and America's Future 1996). Reform efforts that seek increased student achievement reflect the premise that the quality of student learning is directly related to the quality of teaching. The National Commission on Teaching and America's Future captured the crucial nature of this premise by stating, "Teaching quality will make the critical difference not only to the futures of individual children but to America's future as well" (1996, 6).

However, it is not enough to target staff development as a top priority for reform efforts. Leaders who are serious about educational reforms must take into account the nature of teachers as adult learners. All too often staff development does not lead to its ultimate goal—transfer or change in teachers' classroom practices. If leaders truly believe that *all* individuals can learn, they also must believe that it is possible to increase the likelihood that training will transfer to classroom practice. The challenge for leaders is to determine the conditions that scaffold the transfer of training to classroom practice and adopt practices that foster and support those conditions.

What are those conditions? A review of literature on the nature of transfer, teacher efficacy, school culture, and effective staff development practices leads to the premise that the interaction of five conditions encourages and supports the transfer of training to classroom practice: (1) training content linked to student achievement, (2) teacher's sense of efficacy, (3) strong, positive school culture, (4) elements of effective training, and (5) coaching or follow-up.

The Nature of Transfer

"Transfer refers to the effect of learning one kind of material or skill on the ability to learn something new" (Joyce, Weil, and Showers 1992, 386). In essence, transfer and mastery are synonymous. To master a new teaching skill, a teacher needs to develop proficiency in the skill and attain executive control of the skill. Executive control takes place when a teacher understands the purpose and rationale of a skill and knows how to adapt the skill to varied content, particular students, and other instructional strategies. In other words, a teacher has acquired executive control of a skill when he or she is able to use the skill appropriately with ease and adapt it to his or her students and classroom setting.

As maintained by Joyce and Showers, "The positive, cumulative transfer of learned teaching skills and strategies to classroom practice is enormously complex. Newly acquired skills must be integrated into an existing repertoire of skills and knowledge" (1981, 167). In order to achieve executive control, teachers must understand the purpose and rationale of the skill, adjust the skill to their students, apply the skill to subject matter, modify or develop instructional materials, organize students, and integrate the skill with other instructional strategies (Joyce, Weil, and Showers 1992). Marini and Genereux further explained the complexity of transfer by stating that transfer is dependent on the learner's ability to readily access required resources and recognize appropriate transfer situations and the learner's motivation to take advantage of transfer opportunities. These authors also noted that "the requirements of any transfer task include content/conceptual knowledge, procedural/strategic knowledge, and appropriate dispositions" (1995, 3). The nature of transfer affects the ease with which a teacher masters these requirements and achieves executive control of a new skill.

There are two kinds of transfer to classroom practice: horizontal and vertical transfer. Horizontal transfer occurs when a teacher uses a newly learned strategy in his or her classroom the same way that it was taught in training. Vertical transfer occurs when a person makes significant adjustments in applying new learning to his or her particular situation. Vertical transfer is more likely when the context of training and the classroom situation differ significantly, a given drill differs from one's existing repertoire and cannot easily be integrated, or additional learning or understanding is needed to assume executive control of training (Joyce, Weil, and Showers 1992).

The important difference between horizontal and vertical transfer is the amount of learning and adjustment that takes place in order for a teacher to use a new skill with ease in the classroom. If the use of a new skill requires little disruption of existing classroom patterns and only a minimal need for additional learning or adjustment, executive control is relatively easy. Such would be the case for horizontal transfer. But, if the use of a new skill in the classroom differs significantly from the context in which it was taught and requires the teacher to engage in additional learning and make adjustments, executive control will be more difficult. In this case the teacher must vertically transfer what has been learned to classroom practice. Achieving executive control is more difficult when vertical transfer must take place.

Fogarty (1995) described transfer in terms of a continuum. Six stages, or phases, range from near transfer to far transfer. Near transfer is similar to horizontal transfer in that learning is applied to a similar situation, whereas far transfer presumes that learning is carried over to a very different situation. To clarify, an example of near transfer is learning to drive a car and transferring that skill to driving a truck. The situations are quite similar. An example of far transfer is learning about fractions and transferring that learning to halving or doubling a recipe. Both situations are quite dissimilar, and the transfer is far removed from the initial learning.

A closer look at the six levels of transfer—overlooking, duplicating, replicating, integrating, mapping, and innovating—indicates clear differentiation among them. (See Figure 1.) Based on the learning situation, transfer may intentionally or unintentionally be overlooked, simply duplicated just as it was learned, or replicated by retaining much of the way something was learned but adapting it to fit a new situation. At the next levels, transfer may be subtly integrated into the learner's existing repertoire with an increased consciousness of the learning and how it fits into context, strategically mapped into other situations with an explicit intent to use the new learning, or elaborated and enhanced far beyond the original idea.

SITUATIONAL DISPOSITIONS TOWARD TRANSFER

		Does the learner:	
SIMPLE	OVERLOOK:	Miss appropriate opportunities; persist in former ways?	NEAR
SIMPLE	DUPLICATE:	Perform the drill exactly as practiced; duplicate with no change; copy?	NEAR
SIMPLE	REPLICATE:	Tailor, but apply knowledge only in similar situations; produce work that all looks alike?	NEAR
COMPLEX	INTEGRATE:	Subtly combine knowledge with other ideas and situations; use information with raised consciousness?	FAR
COMPLEX	MAP:	Carry a strategy to another content and into life situations; associate?	FAR
COMPLEX	INNOVATE:	Invent; take ideas beyond the initial conception; take risks; diverge?	FAR

FIGURE 1

From Robin Fogarty, "The Most Significant Outcome." In *Best Practices for the Learner-Centered Classroom* (Arlington Heights, IL: IRI/SkyLight Training and Publishing, 1995), p. 274.

The following chart describes Fogarty's phases of transfer through a metaphor of birds. (See Figure 2.) Each of the six phases is depicted in the chart with specific examples of transfer for teachers in training.

An additional consideration is what Bereiter referred to as "situated cognition." This view is based on investigations of people learning in real-life situations and proposes that "people learn by entering ongoing 'communities of practice'" (1995, 29). In other words, the natural way in which learning or transfer takes place is not in formal settings. The real learning that teachers must experience will not take place at the training site; transfer will occur only within a "natural setting"—the teachers' classrooms.

TEACHER LEVELS OF TRANSFER

Ollie
the Head-in-the-sand Ostrich
OVERLOOKS

Does nothing; unaware of relevance and misses appropriate applications; overlooks intentionally or unintentionally. (Resists)

"Great session, but this won't work with my kids or content" or "I chose not to use __ because..."

Dan
the Drilling Woodpecker
DUPLICATES

Drills and practices exactly as presented; Drill! Drill! Then stops; uses as an activity rather than as a strategy; duplicates. (Copies)

"Could I have a copy of that transparency?"

Laura
the Look-alike Penguin
REPLICATES

Tailors to kids and content, but applies to similar content; all look alike; does not transfer into new situations; replicates. (Differentiates)

"I use the web for every character analysis."

Jonathan
Livingston Seagull
INTEGRATES

Raised consciousness; acute awareness; deliberate refinement; integrates subtly with existing repertoire. (Combines)

"I haven't used any of your ideas, but I'm wording my questions carefully. I've always done this, but I'm doing more of it."

Cathy
the Carrier Pigeon
MAPS

Consciously transfers ideas to various situations, contents; carries strategy as part of available repertoire; maps. (Associates)

"I use the webbing strategy in everything."

Samantha
the Soaring Eagle
INNOVATES

Innovates; flies with an idea; takes it into action beyond the initial conception; creates enhances, invents; risks. (Diverges)

"You have changed my teaching forever. I can never go back to what I used to do. I know too much. I'm too excited."

FIGURE 2

From James Bellanca and Robin Fogarty, *Blueprints for Thinking in the Cooperative Classroom* (Palatine, IL: IRI/Skylight Publishing, 1991), p. 273.

Teachers teach in a world that is characterized by diversity. Thus, it is unlikely that most staff development training can be horizontally transferred to classroom practice. In most instances, teachers must adjust new strategies to meet the needs of *their* students in *their* school communities, with *their* resources, and with *their* existing repertoires of strategies. Given the complex nature of most attempts to transfer training to classroom practice, leaders could more effectively support such attempts by identifying conditions that encourage transfer and ascertaining the implications for leadership.

Conditions That Encourage Transfer of Training to Classroom Practice

Change is multidimensional. Although many factors can hinder the successful transfer of change, most unsuccessful attempts can be attributed primarily to two encompassing factors: the inappropriateness of the change being initiated and failure to consider the dynamic and complex nature of change (Fullan and Stiegelbauer 1991).

Educators must "selectively abandon" (Costa 1991) those reforms that are not responsive to the *particular* needs of the individuals who comprise each learning community. If there is not an optimal match between identified needs and the considered innovation, then the reform is doomed from the start. Thus, any reform endeavor, whether accomplished through staff development or through other means, must reflect careful consideration of whether the innovation is appropriate for the explicit conditions in which it must be implemented. Otherwise, it is unlikely that transfer will take place.

Showers, Joyce, and Bennett advised educators to contemplate the complexity of change in determining the elements of effective staff development. They warned that "to reach toward knowledge and interpret it for policymakers and educators" (1987, 80) we must consider a number of variables at the same time:

people, social context, training components, and degrees of implementation. That is, staff development that sustains transfer is dependent upon a number of conditions that interact with one another. When multiple variables are considered in the implementation of staff development, there is greater likelihood that transfer will take place.

What are these variables? Several key trends or themes have emerged from the research and serve as the basis for identifying and expanding upon five conditions that will promote transfer of staff development to practice. A predominate theme is that the success of staff development will be judged by whether it leads to increased student achievement (Sparks 1994). This implies one condition for the transfer of staff development to practice—training content must be such that it will lead to student achievement. Another theme reflected in the research is that staff development must reverberate an understanding of *"the teacher as learner, leader, and colleague"* (Lieberman and Miller 1991, vii [italics added]) in shaping a learning community, one that reflects growth from practice. This idea communicates that teachers' sense of efficacy shapes and is shaped by how they instruct students. Moreover, teachers' instructional practices are influenced not only by the knowledge received through professional development initiatives but also by how the school's culture supports their attempts to engage new practices. A dynamic relationship exists between teacher efficacy and school culture and suggests that both are important conditions for the transfer of training to classroom practice. The current research and emphasis on *constructivism* is a theme that promotes the idea that staff development should train teachers to use constructivist approaches by *modeling* constructivist techniques (Sparks 1994). This implies that two additional conditions—elements of effective training and follow-up—encourage transfer. Last, the idea of *systems thinking,* which recognizes the complex and dynamic relationship among organizational components, impacts the conceptualization of effective staff development (Sparks 1994). It places the five conditions in the context of a cohesive whole that is maintained by how all interact with one another.

Training Content That Is Linked to Student Achievement

The focus of all professional interaction should be student learn-ing. Indeed, "student learning outcomes should provide the start-ing point for *all* school improvement and staff development efforts" (Guskey and Sparks 1996, 37). In recent years, much research has been conducted to determine factors that encour-age student achievement. Staff development content needs to focus on those factors. Content that is positively linked to student achievement focuses on child development, student diversity, research-based effective teaching strategies, curriculum study, studies of effective schools and teachers, classroom management, family involvement, student assessment, and guidance concerns (Joyce and Showers 1995; National Staff Development Council 1995; National Staff Development Council and National Associa-tion of Elementary School Principals 1995; and National Staff Development Council and National Association of Secondary School Principals 1995).

It is especially important that staff development content con-centrates on research-based teaching strategies. Recently cogni-tive scientists have recognized that there is a pedagogy of content that impacts the teaching and learning process. The pedagogy of content is concerned with how each content area is comprised of a structure of knowledge, skills, and dispositions that must be considered in providing effective learning opportunities. As Shulman argued, it is important for a teacher to know

> the structures of subject matter, the principles of conceptual organization, and the principles of inquiry that help answer two kinds of questions in each field: What are the important ideas and skills in this domain? and How are new ideas added and deficient ones dropped by those who produced knowledge in this area? (1987, 9)

Much attention has been given to the knowledge base that teachers must possess, represent, and transfer to their students in order for them to achieve. But knowledge base alone is not enough. Shulman maintained that teachers also need pedagogical content knowledge, a "knowledge of the most useful forms of representation of [those] ideas, the most powerful analogies, illustrations, examples, explanations, and demonstrations—in a word, the ways of representing and formulating the subject that make it comprehensible to others" (1986, 9). Thus, effective staff development content integrates both teaching pedagogy and content knowledge. In this way teachers can enhance their content knowledge while learning strategies that will be more effective in teaching students specific content.

There is an additional reason to ensure that staff development content is linked substantively to research on effective teaching and learning. Research-based practices will more likely lead to student achievement; thus, a positive cause-effect cycle is initiated as teachers see that implementing new ideas makes a positive difference in student achievement and increased student learning encourages teachers to continue new practices (Guskey 1985; Lieberman and Miller 1991; McLaughlin 1991; Showers, Joyce, and Bennett 1987). Teachers who see that implementing new ideas makes a difference in student achievement are more inclined to continue future learning by implementing additional new ideas.

The Teacher's Sense of Efficacy

Sarason said, "Educational change depends on what teachers do and think—it's as simple and complex as that" (Fullan and Stiegelbauer 1991, 117). Teacher knowledge and practices are the primary influences impacting student achievement. Therefore, to increase student learning, staff development must somehow alter teachers' knowledge and classroom practices. It has been found that all teachers are capable of gaining new skills and knowledge and transferring the new learning to classroom practice (Sparks 1986; Showers, Joyce, and Bennett 1987; Joyce, Bennett, and Rolheiser-Bennett 1990). However, a variety of factors influences the extent to which teachers transfer what is introduced through training. One condition that influences whether transfer takes place is a teacher's sense of efficacy, or "the extent to which the teacher believes he or she has the capacity to affect student performance" (Guskey 1994, 628). Guskey indicated that teacher efficacy is a multidimensional concept that reflects a teacher's belief that all students can learn, the belief that he or she is capable of learning a new skill, and the teacher's beliefs about the extent that external factors, such as home environment, have on student learning.

There is a connection between teachers' growth and their self-esteem. In a research synthesis of studies on staff development, Showers, Joyce, and Bennett found that "competent teachers with high self-esteem usually benefit more from training than their less competent, less confident colleagues" (1987, 79). Moreover, a study conducted by McKibbon and Joyce (1980) found that teachers with a positive sense of efficacy were seven times more likely to transfer training than those with low self-esteem. McLaughlin (1991) reiterated that the most powerful teacher characteristic to influence continuation of innovations is the teacher's sense of efficacy.

This sense of efficacy is intrinsically related to concerns about student achievement. Numerous studies support the inseparability of concerns about teachers and concerns about student achievement (Guskey 1985; Lieberman and Miller 1991; McLaughlin 1991; Showers, Joyce, and Bennett 1987). Lieberman and Miller emphasized, "We cannot overstate the importance of teacher-student interactions. When the rewards from these interactions are plenty, teachers are energized and they thrive. When the rewards from these interactions are diminished, teachers lose that part of themselves that is most self-sustaining and most central to the well-being of the profession" (1991, 101). Simply put, the chief rewards of teaching are derived from students.

In large part, a teacher's sense of *efficacy* is related to *motivation*. Sergiovanni (1992) stated that three conditions are critical for motivation. Staff members are most likely to be motivated when they (1) experience meaningfulness from what they are doing, (2) sense responsibility for the outcomes, and (3) receive knowledge of the results of their efforts. Research reinforces the link between motivation and efficacy by indicating that a teacher's efficacy depends on his or her belief that a strategy will make a difference in students *and* the teacher's belief that he or she is capable of learning the strategy. To summarize, an individual is more likely to attempt new practices to the extent he or she is motivated to do so. A sense of meaningfulness and responsibility is related to one's sense of efficacy and impacts one's motivation.

Research regarding teacher efficacy and motivation suggests a departure from traditional premises about staff development that sustains transfer to practice. Traditionally, staff development focused on first changing teacher beliefs and attitudes. It was perceived that such changes would lead to changes in classroom practices and thus increase student learning. However, more current research indicates that "significant change in teachers' attitudes and beliefs takes place *after* student learning outcomes have changed" (Guskey 1985, 57).

For example, once a teacher notices evidence of increased student achievement (e.g., fewer failures) with the introduction of cooperative learning, the teacher is more likely to begin thinking about cooperative learning in the classroom as an integral strategy for learning. The beliefs about classroom practice start to change.

A change in beliefs is dependent upon evidence of change in students. Thus, a chain of events is put into place. Evidence of change in students leads to sustained change in practices. As teachers feel empowered by what they are doing, they gain a sense of efficacy.

The relationship between teacher efficacy and transfer is evident when one considers the many and varied adaptations that teachers must make to transfer training to actual classroom practice. Because of the diverse nature of existing teacher repertoires, students, and classroom settings, most training requires additional learning and complex adaptations. The result is that most teachers experience considerable discomfort when attempting a new strategy. This discomfort is both the *result* of new learning and is a *prerequisite* for learning. Unfortunately, many teachers who experience discomfort, feel awkward, or are not immediately

successful when attempting a new skill or strategy have a ten-
dency to discontinue the new practice. It is only through frequent
use of a new practice that teachers overcome the sense of
discomfort and gain executive control. However, as Joyce, Weil,
and Showers stated, "Only a small percentage (about 5 to 10 percent) of the teachers who had learned teaching strategies new to
their repertoires were able to handle the discomfort without
assistance" (1992, 394).

Times of discomfort can be times of growth. Leaders who provide administrative support can make a crucial difference in
determining whether transfer takes place. As teachers who do
not possess a strong sense of efficacy see that they *can learn* and
effectively *use* new strategies to increase student achievement,
their sense of efficacy increases as well as their motivation to
implement new leanings. Self-actualized teachers are more likely
to take risks and endure the discomfort felt when using new strategies and knowledge as they feel more efficacious in their ability
to increase their students' learning. But even these teachers can
benefit from support.

A Strong, Positive School Culture

Emerging from research is the call for an integrated system of
staff development, one that unifies individual and organizational
growth, provides equilibrium, and scaffolds growth through
change. A strong, positive school culture provides the foundation
for such a system.

Culture is a concept borrowed from anthropologists that is used
to describe and differentiate societies. In recent years, the term
has been applied to describing organizations, such as businesses
and schools. Deal and Peterson suggested that "the culture of an
organization can influence its productivity and there is reason to
believe that the same cultural dimensions that account for high
performance in business account for high achievement in schools"
(1990, 9).

A review of several definitions of culture provides a basis for
understanding how school culture can influence the transfer of

training to practice. Deal defined culture as "an all-encompassing tapestry of meaning . . . the way we do things around here" (1987, 5). Lane added to the understanding of school culture by describing its function as "the organization of prescriptive behaviors around values which are central to the decisions and actions essential to the group's adaptive survival, satisfaction, and goal attainment" (1992, 88).

Learning takes place in a social context, and the school is the primary unit of educational reform. The extent to which a school supports Sergiovanni's and Starratt's (1993) concept of a *learning community* is directly related to *how* the school's culture defines the social organization in which learning can take place. The learning community concept communicates that learning is an ageless, lifelong pursuit; thus, teachers, students, administrators, and other community members can learn from one another and can benefit from purposeful interactions that are focused on achievement. A reciprocal relationship exists between school culture and staff development. The social context impacts *how* teachers implement knowledge or strategies introduced through staff development (Showers and Bennett, 1987). Moreover, staff development can shape the school's culture.

A strong, positive culture is one in which "staff members clearly identify with the school's values, and the values support norms that are good for children" (Gonder and Hymes 1994, 32). School culture either *encourages* or *discourages* teachers' continued growth toward habits of mind and practices that increase student achievement. As stated by Wood, "A positive, healthy school climate that includes trust, open communication, and peer support for changes in practice is essential for successful staff development" (1989, 27). School culture provides the bonding force for faculty cohesiveness and supports reform implementation. Teachers who typically are isolated from one another become members of teams that communicate and collaborate to improve student achievement.

The principal plays a significant role in shaping a school culture that supports effective staff development and promotes transfer. Saphier and King provided guidelines for building a school culture that supports growth. They suggested that principals shape these twelve cultural norms: (1) collegiality, (2) experimentation, (3) high expectations, (4) trust and confidence, (5) tangible support, (6) reaching out to knowledge bases, (7) appreciation and recognition, (8) caring, celebration, and humor, (9) involvement in decision making, (10) protection of what is important, (11) traditions, and (12) honest, open communication (1985, 67). These cultural norms describe practices that support the transfer of training to classroom practice as they provide assurance that teachers will not be penalized in their first shaky attempts at new practices. The norms also communicate an expectation that professional growth will occur and support will be given for growth.

Research directly links school culture and the effectiveness of staff development to the leadership provided by the principal. Principals can support individual and collective growth by helping staff members cultivate and preserve a collaborative school culture, supporting technical development and nurturing teacher development, facilitating effective problem solving, and recasting routine administrative activities into teacher development activities (Leithwood 1990, 1992). Lee (1990) advised principals to create communities of learners by modeling and guiding reflective practice, shaping a positive school culture, and providing collaborative working arrangements. The extent to which administrators promote the norms of a strong, positive school culture and the corresponding practices impacts whether teachers receive the support needed to overcome the discomfort experienced in the transfer process.

Elements of Effective Training

For more than twenty years a significant amount of research has accumulated concerning elements of training and follow-up. A meta-analysis of over 200 research studies on effective staff development components indicated that the location of the training, its scheduling, and the role of the trainer did not seem to make a significant difference—what mattered most was training design (Killion and Harrison 1988; Showers, Joyce, and Bennett 1987).

The most effective training design incorporates four components: (1) presentation of theory or rationale, (2) demonstration or modeling of skill or concept, (3) practice of skill or concept under simulated conditions, and (4) feedback (Joyce, Showers, and Bennett 1987; Joyce and Showers 1980, 1983, 1995; Sparks 1986). Teachers who participate in training that utilizes these four elements are more than twice as likely to gain the targeted knowledge than if presentations alone are employed (Joyce and Showers 1995). However, the combination of these four components during training is not enough to guarantee transfer.

Coaching or Follow-up

In order to accomplish transfer, a fifth component, coaching, should be included as an essential element of training (Brandt 1987; Joyce and Showers 1981). Coaching provides opportunities for participants to discuss, use, and adapt a *particular* strategy, in their *particular* classrooms, with their *particular* students. Such adaptation is required for executive control. As many teachers experience discomfort when learning something new, coaching can provide nonthreatening assistance to help them overcome their discomfort and successfully adapt new learnings to their classrooms.

Coaching is "the provision of on-site personal support and technical assistance for teachers" (Baker and Showers 1984, 1). Coaching can be provided by peers, experts, administrators, or supervisors as long as there is a clear distinction between coaching and the evaluation process. Coaching should include from ten to fifteen cycles of pre-observation, observation, and post-observation.

Joyce and Showers were the first to use "coaching" as a term for follow-up to training. Since they introduced coaching in the early 1980s, numerous forms of coaching have been conceptualized and implemented. Garmston (1987) identified three forms of peer coaching: (1) technical coaching that follows staff training, (2) collegial coaching that helps teachers refine self-identified practices, and (3) challenge coaching that focuses on problem solving. Garmston, Linder, and Whitaker (1993) suggested a fourth form—cognitive coaching, which encourages teachers to explore the thinking behind their practices and can be used in combination with other forms of coaching. Lee (1990) suggested that principals provide their staffs with opportunities to engage in collaborative inquiry. Collaborative inquiry can be conducted in groups of varying sizes and focuses on questions that encourage teachers to examine, speculate, hypothesize, and experiment for the sake of increased awareness and self-improvement.

Whatever form is used, coaching serves several functions to extend training and encourage transfer. Coaching provides companionship, technical feedback, analysis of application, and adaptation to students (Joyce and Showers 1983). Coached teachers are more likely to practice new strategies, develop greater skill, and use strategies more appropriately than uncoached teachers. Teachers who engage in some form of follow-up or coaching also exhibit greater long-term retention of knowledge and skill of learned strategies. Coached teachers also demonstrate more understanding of the varied purposes and use of new strategies and thus teach the new models to their students on a more frequent basis (Joyce and Showers 1995). This benefit reflects that coaching provides the support teachers need to vertically transfer training to practice and gain executive control of a skill.

Research conducted by Stallings confirmed elements of staff development follow-up that lead to transfer. Stallings's quest to improve students' reading achievement led to an examination of elements necessary for effective staff development. Stallings found that teachers are more inclined to change their behavior and continue to use new ideas when they do the following:

1. Become aware of a need for improvement through an analysis of their own observation profile,
2. Make a written commitment to attempt new ideas the day after training,
3. Modify the workshop ideas for their own classroom and school,
4. Try the ideas and evaluate the effect,
5. Observe in each others' classrooms and analyze their data,

6. Report their success or failure to their group,
7. Discuss problems and solutions regarding individual students and instructional situations,
8. Are involved in a wide variety of training approaches such as modeling, simulations, observations, critiquing videotapes, presenting at professional meetings, and
9. Learn to set new goals for professional growth (1988, 4).

These practices require the use of reflection, collaboration, observation, and feedback—the attributes of coaching.

The success of coaching can be attributed to its collaborative nature as well as to its cognitive function. Research indicates that important components of teaching practices are cognitive in nature and that "what the teacher thinks about teaching determines what the teacher does when teaching" (Showers, Joyce, and Bennett 1987, 79). Basically, three aspects of thinking influence a teacher's classroom performance: (1) the teacher's planning before and after instruction, (2) the teacher's thoughts and decisions while teaching, and (3) the teacher's theories and beliefs (Clark and Peterson 1986). "Each person maintains a cognitive map" (Garmston, Linder, and Whitaker 1993, 57), and coaching helps the teacher to unfold that map to improve teaching and learning.

The power of coaching increases when the entire school focuses on training with peer-coaching teams as follow-up. Joyce and Showers (1995) showed the relation between the pattern of participation and level of implementation. Participation by individuals without peer structures resulted in 5 to 10 percent implementation. Participation by peer-coaching teams from a variety of schools averaged 75 percent implementation or better. And schools where the entire faculty participated in training, with peer-coaching teams for follow-up, showed the highest level of implementation—90 to 100 percent. These figures reflect a link between staff development, school culture, coaching, and transfer. When coaching is used as follow-up to *schoolwide* staff development, the likelihood of implementation is the greatest.

A Conceptualization of Five Conditions That Foster and Support Transfer

Research supports the premise that five conditions foster and support the transfer of training to classroom practice: (1) training content that is linked to student achievement, (2) the teacher's sense
of efficacy, (3) a strong, positive school culture, (4) elements of
effective training, and (5) coaching or follow-up. When these conditions are present, they form an interactive whole that consti-
tutes effective staff development. (See Figure 3.)

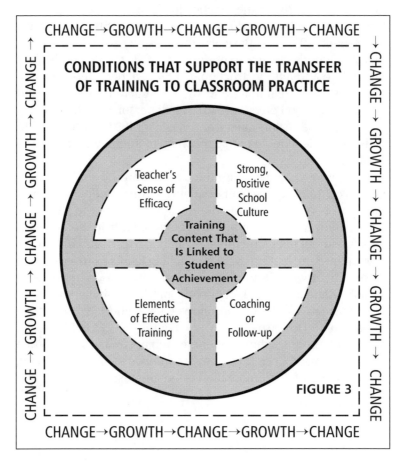

The conceptualization of conditions that promote transfer begins with a focal point of training content that is linked to student achievement. This condition provides the unifying connection among the other four conditions. The centricity of this condition communicates that staff development must be based on substantive content if it is to positively impact the teaching and learning process. Its primacy also indicates that the effects of teacher efficacy, a strong, positive school culture, training elements, and coaching will be realized only to the extent that the content of staff development is linked to student achievement. Training content that is linked to student achievement interacts with the other four conditions to (1) increase the success rate of teachers in improving student achievement and encourage a strong sense of teacher efficacy, (2) focus collaborative school efforts on increasing student achievement and shaping a strong school culture, (3) incorporate effective training design, and (4) provide coaching techniques that build collaborative relationships and render support to improvement efforts. A dynamic relationship exists among the five conditions. They are both interrelated *and* integrated. Leaders should consider the synergistic relationship among these five conditions in encouraging the transfer of training to classroom practice.

Implications for School Leaders

School leaders have the power to promote learning communities in which student and staff growth are intertwined explicitly. Administrators can nurture teacher growth by relentlessly insisting on practices that support teachers' efforts to increase their repertoire of instructional skills and practices. In this endeavor, leaders can take concrete steps to promote the five conditions that support the transfer of staff development to student achievement.

First, school leaders can focus on training content that is known to increase student achievement. Thus, staff development initiatives need to reflect a careful analysis of student needs, concentrate on developing *research-based* skills and knowledge, and communicate to teachers *how* these skills and knowledge will increase student achievement. Moreover, strategies need to be taught in the context of content knowledge. The extent to which staff development content is linked to improved student achievement determines whether transfer takes place.

Second, leaders must nurture an environment in which teachers have opportunities to experience efficacy. One way this can be accomplished is by communicating an explicit link between staff development content and increased student achievement. Also, leaders should articulate a clear plan as to how support and follow-up will be provided during implementation of a new practice. The administrative support that leaders provide when teachers learn new skills can make a crucial difference in whether a teacher believes he or she is capable of learning and using a new strategy effectively. A teacher's belief in the ability to change is vital to his or her desire to persevere. Administrators also need to provide specific, consistent, and regular feedback concerning the impact of staff development on students and staff members. Such feedback reveals teachers' responsibilities in student learning and discloses the fruits of teachers' efforts. Administrative practices such as these highlight that training makes a difference in teacher *and* student learning. When teachers see that what *they* are doing makes a difference in student achievement, *they* experience a sense of efficacy that impacts future efforts.

A third way that leaders can encourage transfer is by establishing practices that foster the twelve cultural norms identified by Saphier and King (1985). Particular attention should be given to establishing administrative practices that promote these norms: (1) collegiality, (2) experimentation, (3) tangible support, (4) reaching out to the knowledge bases about teaching, and (5) honest, open communication. These five cultural norms are crucial for effective staff development and provide the framework upon which a strong, positive school culture can be built—the third condition that promotes transfer.

School leaders can sustain the fourth and fifth conditions by ensuring that the elements of effective training and coaching are implemented for all training endeavors and by providing the

resources to support staffs' efforts. Personnel, material, and scheduling resources need to be considered. Also, school leaders need
to ensure that specific goals are articulated and select coaching
models that reflect the articulated goals.

Perhaps the most significant way that administrators can provide a discernible glimpse of the power these five conditions have
in fostering transfer is by *demonstrating* a commitment to learning. Leaders must be willing to reveal their own desire to grow
professionally *and* the explicit steps they are taking in that growth
process. Leaders must *model* a willingness to try, evaluate, modify,
and try again—the same behaviors required of teachers for transfer of training to classroom practice. As Dewey wrote, "The self is
not ready-made but something in continuous formation through
choice of action" (1916, 408). The extent to which all educators
commit themselves to this ideal and the extent to which the five
described conditions are manifested in our educational settings
will determine the degree to which transfer among *all* learners
will be realized.

Bibliography

Ackland, Robert. "A Review of the Peer Coaching Literature." *Journal of Staff Development* 12 (1991): 22–27.

Baker, R. G., and Beverly Showers. "The Effects of a Coaching Strategy on Teachers' Transfer of Training to Classroom Practice: A Six-Month Follow-up Study." Paper presented at the annual meeting of the American Educational Research Association, New Orleans, LA, 1984.

Bereiter, Carl. "A Dispositional View of Transfer." In *Teaching for Transfer,* edited by Anne McKeough, Judy L. Lupart, and Anthony Marini. Mahwah, NJ: Lawrence Erlbaum Associates, 1995.

Brandt, Ronald S. "On Teaching Coaching Teachers: A Conversation with Bruce Joyce." *Educational Leadership* 44 (1987): 12–16.

Clark, C. M., and P. L. Peterson. "Teachers' Thought Processes." In *Handbook of Research on Teaching,* edited by Merlin C. Wittrock. 3rd ed. New York: Macmillan, 1986.

Costa, Art. "The School as a Home for the Mind: Leadership as an Environmental Protection Agency." Presentation at the annual conference of the Association for Supervision and Curriculum Development, Williamsburg, VA, December 1996.

———. "Orchestrating the Second Wave." *Cogitare* 5, no. 2 (1991).

Cuban, Larry. "A Fundamental Puzzle of School Reform." *Phi Delta Kappan* 69 (1988): 341–344.

Deal, Terrance E. "The Culture of Schools." In *Leadership: Examining the Elusive,* edited by L. T. Shieve and M. B. Schoenheit. Alexandria, VA: Association for Supervision and Curriculum Development, 1987.

Deal, Terrance E., and K. D. Peterson. *The Principal's Role in Guiding School Culture.* Washington, DC: U.S. Department of Education, Office of Educational Research and Improvement, 1990.

Dewey, John. *Democracy and Education.* New York: Macmillan, 1916.

Doyle, W. "Curriculum and Pedagogy." In *Handbook of Research on Curriculum,* edited by P. W. Jackson. New York: Macmillan, 1992.

Fogarty, Robin. "From Training to Transfer: The Role of Creativity in Adult Learners." Ph.D. diss., Loyola University of Chicago, 1989.

———. "The Most Significant Outcome." In *Best Practices for the Learner-Centered Classroom.* Arlington Heights, IL: IRI/SkyLight Training and Publishing, 1995.

Fullan, Michael G. "Staff Development, Innovation, and Instructional Development." In *Changing School Culture Through Staff Development,* edited by Bruce Joyce. Alexandria, VA: Association for Supervision and Curriculum Development, 1990.

Fullan, Michael G., and Suzanne Stiegelbauer. *The New Meaning of Educational Change.* New York: Teachers College Press, 1991.

Garmston, Robert J. "How Administrators Support Peer Coaching." *Educational Leadership* 44 (1987): 18–26.

Garmston, Robert J., Christina Linder, and Jan Whitaker. "Reflections on Cognitive Coaching." *Educational Leadership* 51 (1993): 57–61.

Glass, J. Conrad. "Components That Promote Transfer of Learning to the Classroom: Are They Present in Staff Development Activities for Teachers?" *Educational Research Quarterly* 15 (1992): 35–44.

Glatthorn, Allan A. "Cooperative Professional Development: Peer-Centered Options for Teacher Growth." *Educational Leadership* 45 (1987): 31–35.

Gonder, Peggy O., and Donald Hymes. *Improving School Climate and Culture.* Arlington, VA: American Association of School Administrators, 1994.

Goodlad, John I. *A Place Called School.* New York: McGraw-Hill, 1984.

Gordon, Stephen P., James F. Nolan, and Vito A. Forlenza. "Peer Coaching: A Cross-Site Comparison." *Journal of Personnel Evaluation in Education* 9 (1995): 69–91.

Guskey, Thomas R. "Staff Development and Teacher Change." *Educational Leadership* 42 (1985): 57–59.

———. "Teacher Efficacy: A Study of Construct Dimensions." *American Educational Research Journal* 31 (1994): 627–641.

Guskey, Thomas R., and Dennis Sparks. "Exploring the Relationship Between Staff Development and Improvements in Student Learning." *Journal of Staff Development* 17 (1996): 34–38.

Huberman, A. Michael, and Matthew B. Miles. *Innovation up Close.* New York: Plenum, 1984.

Joyce, Bruce, Barrie Bennett, and Carol Rolheiser-Bennett. "The Self-Educating Teacher: Empowering Teachers Through Research." In *Changing School Culture Through Staff Development,* edited by Bruce Joyce. Alexandria, VA: Association for Supervision and Curriculum Development, 1990.

Joyce, Bruce, and Beverly Showers. "Improving Inservice Training: Messages of Research." *Educational Research* 37 (1980): 379–385.

———. "Transfer of Training: The Contribution of 'Coaching'." *Journal of Education* 163 (1981): 163–172.

———. *Power in Staff Development Through Research on Training.* Alexandria, VA: Association for Supervision and Curriculum Development, 1983.

———. *Student Achievement Through Staff Development: Fundamentals of School Renewal.* 2nd ed. White Plains, NY: Longman Publishing, 1995.

Joyce, Bruce, Marsha Weil, and Beverly Showers. *Models of Teaching.* Boston: Allyn and Bacon, 1992.

Killion, J. P., and C. R. Harrison. "Evaluating Training Programs: Three Critical Elements for Success." *Journal of Staff Development* 9 (1988): 34–48.

Landrum, Mary S. "Peer Coaching as Inservice Follow-up." Ph.D. diss., University of Virginia, 1990. Abstract in *Dissertation Abstracts International* 51 (1990): 11A.

Lane, B. A. "Cultural Leaders in Effective Schools: The Builders and Brokers of Excellence." *NASSP Bulletin* 76 (1992): 85–96.

Lee, G. V. *Instructional Leadership as Collaborative Inquiry: Opportunities and Challenges.* Contract No. 400-86-009. Washington, DC: Office of Educational Research and Improvement, 1990.

Leithwood, Kenneth. "The Principal's Role in Teacher Development." In *Changing School Culture Through Staff Development,* edited by Bruce Joyce. Alexandria, VA: Association for Supervision and Curriculum Development, 1990.

———. "The Move Toward Transformational Leadership." *Educational Leadership* 49 (1992): 8–12.

Licklider, B. L. "The Effects of Peer Coaching Cycles on Teacher Use of a Complex Teaching Skill and Teacher's Sense of Efficacy." *Journal of Personnel Evaluation in Education* 9 (1995): 58–68.

Lieberman, Ann, and Lynne Miller. "Revisiting the Social Realities of Teaching." In *Staff Development for Education in the '90s.* New York: Teachers College Press, 1991.

Little, Judith W. "Norms of Collegiality and Experimentation: Workplace Conditions of School Success." *American Educational Research Journal* 19 (1982): 325–340.

Marini, Anthony, and R. Genereux. "The Challenge of Teaching for Transfer." In *Teaching for Transfer,* edited by Anne McKeough, Judy L. Lupart, and Anthony Marini. Mahway, NJ: Lawrence Erlbaum Associates, 1995.

McKibbon, M., and Bruce Joyce. "Psychological States and Staff Development." *Theory into Practice* 19 (1980): 248–255.

McLaughlin, M. W. "Enabling Professional Development: What Have We Learned?" In *Staff Development for Education in the '90s,* edited by Ann Lieberman and Lynne Miller. New York: Teachers College Press, 1991.

McLaughlin, M. W., and Lorrie A. Shepard, with Jennifer O'Day. *Improving Education Through Standards-Based Reform.* Stanford, CA: Stanford University, The National Academy of Education, 1995.

Merriam-Webster's Collegiate Dictionary. Springfield, MA: G. and C. Merriam Company, 1980.

Moye, Valerie H. *Influencing Change Through Staff Development.* Manuscript submitted for publication, Williamsburg, VA: The College of William and Mary at Williamsburg, 1996.

National Commission on Teaching and America's Future. *What Matters Most: Teaching for America's Future.* New York: National Commission on Teaching and America's Future, 1996.

National Staff Development Council. *Standards for Staff Development: Middle School Edition.* Oxford, OH: National Staff Development Council, 1995.

National Staff Development Council and National Association of Elementary School Principals. *Standards for Staff Development: Elementary School Edition.* Oxford, OH: National Staff Development Council, 1995.

National Staff Development Council and National Association of Secondary School Principals. *Standards for Staff Development: Secondary School Edition.* Oxford, OH: National Staff Development Council, 1995.

Nolan, James F., and Keith Hillkirk. "The Effects of Reflective Coaching Project for Veteran Teachers." *Journal of Curriculum and Supervision* 7 (1991): 62–76.

Richardson, J. "Teacher Knowledge, Skills Most Important Influences on Student Learning." *The Developer: Powerful Ideas for Promoting Improvement* (November 1996): 1–4.

Saphier, Jon, and Matthew King. "Good Schools Grow in Strong Cultures." *Educational Leadership* 38 (1985): 66–77.

Sergiovanni, Thomas J. *Moral Leadership: Getting to the Heart of School Improvement.* San Francisco: Jossey-Bass Publishers, 1992.

Sergiovanni, Thomas J., and R. J. Starratt. *Supervision: A Redefinition.* New York: McGraw-Hill, 1993.

Showers, Beverly. *Peer Coaching: A Strategy for Facilitating Transfer of Training.* Eugene: University of Oregon, Center for Educational Policy and Management, 1984.

Showers, Beverly, Bruce Joyce, and Barrie Bennett. "Synthesis of Research on Staff Development: A Framework for Future Study and a State-of-the-Art Analysis." *Educational Leadership* 45 (1987): 77–87.

Shulman, Lee. "Those Who Understand: Knowledge Growth in Teaching." *Educational Leadership* 15 (1986): 4–14.

———. "Knowledge and Teaching: Foundations of the New Reform." *Harvard Educational Review* 57 (1987): 1–22.

Sparks, Dennis. "A Paradigm Shift in Staff Development." *Journal of Staff Development* 15 (1994): 26–29.

Sparks, Dennis, and Susan Loucks-Horsley. *Five Models of Staff Development for Teachers.* Oxford, OH: National Staff Development Council, 1990.

Sparks, Georgea M. "The Effectiveness of Alternative Training Activities in Changing Teacher Practices." *American Educational Research Journal* 23 (1986): 217–225.

Stallings, J. A. "The Houston Teaching Academy: A Professional Development School." Paper presented at the annual conference of the American Educational Research Association, New Orleans, LA, 1988.

Wood, Fred H. "Organizing and Managing School-Based Staff Development." In *Staff Development: A Handbook of Effective Practices,* edited by S. D. Caldwell. Oxford, OH: National Staff Development Council, 1989.

There are
one-story intellects,
two-story intellects, and three-story
intellects with skylights. All fact collectors, who
have no aim beyond their facts, are one-story men. Two-story men
compare, reason, generalize, using the labors of the fact collectors as
well as their own. Three-story men idealize, imagine,
predict—their best illumination comes from
above, through the skylight.

—*Oliver Wendell*

Holmes